TIGER ATTACK

by Lisa Owings

BELLWETHER MEDIA · MINNEAPOLIS, MN

Are you ready to take it to the extreme?
Torque books thrust you into the action-
packed world of sports, vehicles, mystery,
and adventure. These books may include
dirt, smoke, fire, and dangerous stunts.
WARNING : read at your own risk.

Library of Congress Cataloging-in-Publication Data

Owings, Lisa.
 Tiger attack / by Lisa Owings.
   p. cm. -- (Torque: animal attacks)
 Includes bibliographical references and index.
 Summary: "Engaging images illustrate true tiger attack stories and accompany survival tips. The
combination of high-interest subject matter and light text is intended for students in grades 3 through 7"
--Provided by publisher.
 ISBN 978-1-60014-792-0 (hardcover : alk. paper)
 1. Tiger attacks--Juvenile literature. 2. Tiger--Behavior--Juvenile literature. I. Title.
 QL737.C23O957 2013
 599.75615'3--dc23

                                    2012011226

This edition first published in 2013 by Bellwether Media, Inc.

Printed in the United States of America, North Mankato, MN.

A special thanks to Suzanne Lee for contributing an image.

TABLE OF CONTENTS

Terrible Tigers

The tiger is the largest cat in the world. It may also be the deadliest. A tiger starts hunting when the sun goes down. It lets its meal wander close. Then it launches its massive body at the **prey**. The tiger's 4-inch (10-centimeter) claws tear through flesh. Its teeth sink deep into a soft throat. That throat sometimes belongs to a human.

A tiger can eat up to 60 pounds (27 kilograms) of meat at one time.

Manhunt

Tambun Gediu was hunting in
the Malaysian jungle near his home.
He moved silently after a squirrel.
Soon he brought a **blowpipe** to
his lips. He was just about to shoot
when he noticed another hunter
in the jungle. A hungry tiger had
been **stalking** him. Tambun raced
up a nearby tree, but the huge cat
dragged him to the ground.

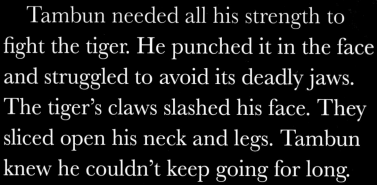

Tambun needed all his strength to fight the tiger. He punched it in the face and struggled to avoid its deadly jaws. The tiger's claws slashed his face. They sliced open his neck and legs. Tambun knew he couldn't keep going for long.

Han, Tambun's wife, heard the tiger's deep roar. The chilling sound came from where her husband was hunting. She knew Tambun was in danger.

Battle Cry

A tiger's roar can be heard up to 2 miles (3.2 kilometers) away.

9

The only weapon Han could find was a wooden soup ladle. She grabbed it and ran into the jungle. There she saw the tiger **mauling** her husband. Han screamed and rushed toward the beast. She whacked it across the head with her ladle. That blow sent the tiger running. Tambun had to wait ten hours to be treated. He returned home covered in scars, but still alive.

"The tiger would have clawed me to death if my wife had not arrived."
—Tambun Gediu

Tangle with a Tiger

Tarulata walked outside her small home in the Sundarbans. It was early morning and time to feed her chickens. Suddenly a huge animal sprang from the bushes and **pounced** on her. At first she thought it was a large dog. Then she realized it was a Bengal tiger.

The tiger ripped open her chest and tore a chunk out of her thigh. Its claws shredded her face and **scalp**. Tarulata could hardly see through the blood.

Tiger Territory
The Sundarbans is a large, swampy forest in southern Asia. It is one of the only places where tigers are still common.

Somehow Tarulata gathered the strength to fight back. She pushed the beast off with a mighty shove. It splashed into the pond behind her. Tarulata dragged herself into her house. She was safe, but the tiger was still looking for a meal. It crept into the heart of the village to search for other **victims**.

Cruel Killers

Tigers kill more than 50 people each year in the Sundarbans. Attacks have increased in recent years.

"We don't feel safe anymore."
—Surendra Jana,
Sundarbans honey gatherer

15

"You learn to live with the tigers. Even if they cast a shadow of terror all the time."

—Kumar Mali,
Sundarbans fisherman

Villagers had heard Tarulata's struggle. They knew a tiger was among them. A group of men followed a trail of screams and dead **livestock** to the tiger. They trapped the animal with fishing nets until it could be **tranquilized**. Meanwhile, Tarulata was taken to the hospital. She fully recovered, except for her scars and a blind left eye. She will never forget the day she won a fight with a tiger.

Tarulata Mandol

Prevent a Tiger Attack

Tigers usually attack people to protect their cubs or **territory**. Some tigers hunt people for food. It is best to stay out of tiger territory if possible. If not, travel with a group in daylight. Keep your distance if you spot a tiger. Do not run if it comes near. Face the animal and make yourself look as large as possible.

Dinner in Disguise

Tigers usually sneak up on their prey from behind. People who work in tiger territory often wear masks on the backs of their heads to confuse tigers.

Survive a Tiger Attack

If the tiger pounces, try to stay on your feet. Force its paws down. If it opens its jaws, shove your fist into its throat. This triggers the tiger's gag reflex so it cannot bite. You can also pull back on the corners of the tiger's mouth. If you come face-to-face with the beast, bite its sensitive nose. Fight hard and you might be among the lucky few who survive a tiger attack.

Glossary

blowpipe—a weapon used to hunt wild animals; a hunter blows into the pipe to shoot a dart.

livestock—farm animals that people sell or use for chores

mauling—attacking and injuring with deep wounds

pounced—jumped onto and grabbed suddenly

prey—an animal that is hunted by other animals for food

scalp—the skin that covers the top and back of the head

stalking—hunting or tracking a person or animal in a quiet, secret way

territory—the area of land where an animal lives, searches for food, and raises its young

tranquilized—calmed by a drug; sometimes people shoot wild animals with tranquilizer guns to keep both themselves and the animals safe.

victims—people or animals that are hurt, killed, or made to suffer

To Learn More

AT THE LIBRARY

Goldish, Meish. *Siberian Tiger: The World's Biggest Cat.* New York, N.Y.: Bearport Pub., 2010.

Sexton, Colleen. *The Bengal Tiger.* Minneapolis, Minn.: Bellwether Media, 2012.

Woolf, Alex. *Killer Cats.* Mankato, Minn.: Arcturus Pub., 2012.

ON THE WEB

Learning more about tigers is as easy as 1, 2, 3.

1. Go to www.factsurfer.com.

2. Enter "tigers" into the search box.

3. Click the "Surf" button and you will see a list of related Web sites.

With factsurfer.com, finding more information is just a click away.

Index